Durable Limited
Power of Attorney Kit

D1712618

enodare
by Enodare Publishing

Bibliographic data
- International Standard Book Number (ISBN): 978-1-906144-35-7
- Printed in the United States of America
- First Printing: January 2011
-

Published by: Enodare Limited
                         Athlone
                         Co. Westmeath
                         Ireland

Printed and distributed by: International Publishers Marketing
                               22841 Quicksilver Drive
                               Dulles, VA 20166
                               United States of America

For more information, e-mail books@enodare.com.

Warning and Disclaimer

Although precautions have been taken in the preparation of this kit, neither the publisher nor the author assumes any responsibility for errors or omissions. No warranty of fitness is implied. The information is provided on an "as is" basis. The author and the publisher shall have neither liability nor responsibility to any person or entity with respect to any loss or damages (whether arising by negligence or otherwise) arising from the use of or reliance on the information contained in this kit or from the use of the forms/documents accompanying it.

IMPORTANT NOTE

This kit is meant as a general guide to preparing your own durable limited power of attorney. While considerable effort has been made to make this kit as complete and accurate as possible, laws and their interpretation are constantly changing. As such, you are advised to update this information with your own research and/or counsel and to consult with your personal legal, financial and medical advisors before acting on any information contained in this kit.

The purpose of this kit is to educate and entertain. It is not meant to provide legal, financial or medical advice or to create any attorney-client or advisory relationship. The authors and publisher shall have neither liability (whether in negligence or otherwise) nor responsibility to any person or entity with respect to any loss or damage caused or alleged to be caused directly or indirectly by the information or forms contained in this kit or the use of that information or those forms.

ABOUT ENODARE

Enodare, the international self-help legal publisher, was founded in 2000 by lawyers from one of the most prestigious international law firms in the World.

Our aim was simple - to provide access to quality legal information and products at an affordable price.

Our Will Writer software was first published in that year and, following its adaptation to cater for the legal systems of over 30 countries worldwide, quickly drew in excess of 40,000 visitors per month to our website. From this humble start, Enodare has quickly grown to become a leading international estate planning and asset protection self-help publisher with legal titles in the United States, Canada, the United Kingdom, Australia and Ireland.

Our publications provide customers with the confidence and knowledge to help them deal with everyday estate planning issues such as the preparation of a last will and testament, a living trust, a power of attorney, administering an estate and much more.

By providing customers with much needed information and forms, we enable them to place themselves in a position where they can protect both themselves and their families through the use of easy to read legal documents and forward planning techniques.

The Future….

We are always seeking to expand and improve the products and services we offer. However, in order to do this, we need to hear from interested authors and to receive feedback from our customers.

If something isn't clear to you in our publications, please let us know and we'll try to make it clearer in the next edition. If you can't find the answer you want and have a suggestion for an addition to our range, we'll happily look at that too.

USING SELF-HELP KITS

Before using a self-help kit, you need to carefully consider the advantages and disadvantages of doing so – particularly where the subject matter is of a legal or tax related nature.

In writing our self-help kits, we try to provide readers with an overview of the laws in a specific area, as well as some sample documents. While this overview is often general in nature, it provides a good starting point for those wishing to carry out a more detailed review of a topic.

However, unlike an attorney advising a client, we cannot cover every conceivable eventuality that might affect our readers. Within the intended scope of this kit, we can only cover the principal areas in a given topic, and even where we cover these areas, we can still only do so to a moderate extent. To do otherwise would result in the writing of a text book which would be capable of use by legal professionals. This is not what we do.

We try to present useful information and documents that can be used by an average reader with little or no legal knowledge. While our sample documents can be used in the vast majority of cases, everybody's personal circumstances are different. As such, they may not be suitable for everyone. You may have personal circumstances which might impact the effectiveness of these documents or even your desire to use them. The reality is that without engaging an attorney to review your personal circumstances, this risk will always exist. It's for this very reason that you need to consider whether the cost of using a do-it-yourself legal document outweighs the risk that there may be something special about your particular circumstances which might not be taken into account by the sample documents attached to this kit (or indeed any other sample documents).

It goes without saying (we hope) that if you are in any doubt as to whether the documents in this kit are suitable for use in your particular circumstances, you should contact a suitably qualified attorney for advice before using them. Remember the decision to use these documents is yours! We are not advising you in any respect.

In using this kit, you should also take into account the fact that this kit has been written with the purpose of providing a general overview of the laws in the United States. As such, it does not attempt to cover all of the various procedural nuances and specific requirements that may apply from state to state – although we do point some of these out along the way. Rather, in our kit, we try to provide forms which give a fair example of the type of forms which are commonly used in most states. Nevertheless, it remains possible that your state may have specific requirements which have not been taken into account in our forms.

Another thing that you should remember is that the law changes – thousands of new laws are brought into force every day and, by the same token, thousands are repealed or amended every day! As such, it is possible that while you are reading this kit, the law might well have been changed. Let's hope it hasn't but the chance does exist! Needless to say, we take regular steps (including e-mail alerts) to update our customers about any changes to the law. We also ensure that our books and kits are reviewed and revised regularly to take account of these changes.

Anyway, assuming that all of the above is acceptable to you, let's move on to exploring the topic at hand.........durable limited powers of attorney.

TABLE OF CONTENTS

DURABLE LIMITED POWER OF ATTORNEY

What Is a Power of Attorney?

A power of attorney is a legal document by which you can appoint and authorize another person (usually a trusted friend, family member, colleague or adviser) to act on your behalf and to legally bind you in that respect. While most people fail to see the importance of having a power of attorney, there are many compelling reasons why they should be used. Suppose, for example that:

- you are going to be out of the country for an extended period, and need someone trustworthy to manage your business affairs while you're away;

- you wish to acquire property in another state, and you need to authorize a local to sign and lodge documents on your behalf;

- you want someone to manage your real estate for you; or

- you're getting a little bit older and wish to appoint someone you know and trust to make healthcare decisions on your behalf should the day come when you are unable to do so yourself.

A power of attorney can be used to facilitate your needs in each of these scenarios.

The person giving the power of attorney is referred to as the 'donor', 'grantor' or 'principal', while the recipient is called the 'agent', 'attorney-in-fact' or just plain 'attorney' (which doesn't mean they have to be a legal practitioner!).

Types of Powers of Attorney

There are a number of different types of power of attorney all serving different needs and requirements. We'll take a look at some of the main types below.

General Power of Attorney

A 'general power of attorney' is virtually <u>unlimited</u> in scope. It allows your agent to act as your authorized legal representative in relation to the whole cross-section of your legal and financial affairs until such time as that authorization is terminated. In other words, your agent will have full legal authority to make decisions and take actions on your behalf, as if you were taking them yourself. This could, for example, include signing letters and checks, executing contracts, etc!

While you cannot generally limit the scope of the power conferred under a general power of attorney, there are nonetheless some presumed limits to the agent's authority. For example, your agent is not normally permitted to assume any position or office that you might hold, such as the position of employee, company director, trustee, personal representative or indeed many others. Furthermore, an agent cannot execute a will on your behalf (or amend an existing one), take action concerning your marriage or delegate his or her authorization under your power of attorney to a third party, unless expressly authorized to do so in the power of attorney document. An agent is also prevented from making gifts of your assets, other than small gifts that you yourself might have been expected to make having regard to the size of your estate.

It's important to bear in mind that you will remain personally liable for the actions of your agent, so you should grant authorization only to someone you trust implicitly.

A general power of attorney (unless stated to be durable) automatically comes to an end if you become mentally incapacitated or die.

Limited Power of Attorney

A 'limited power of attorney' is very similar to a general power of attorney except that it imposes specific and sometimes substantial limits upon the authorization granted to your agent. This could, for example, be a limit to the scope or duration of the authority granted to him.

Often, people granting powers of attorney limit their agent's authority to completing specific transactions or tasks. For example, you may appoint someone as your agent solely for the purpose of having them sign a document on your behalf but only in a format pre-approved by you and attached to the power of attorney document itself. Alternatively, you can appoint your agent for the sole purpose of dealing with a single task or transaction (such as the sale of a piece of real estate to a specified individual at a specified price). These types of limitations remove a substantial part of the risk associated with granting powers of attorney.

Similar to the position with a general power of attorney, you will remain personally liable for the actions of your agent. In addition, a limited power of attorney (unless stated to be durable) will automatically come to an end if you become mentally incapacitated or die.

Healthcare Power of Attorney

One of the most common forms of power of attorney in use today is the 'medical' or 'healthcare' power of attorney.

A healthcare power of attorney allows you to authorize an agent to make healthcare decisions on your behalf if you are incapacitated and unable to do so. The authorization conferred on your agent can cover any form of healthcare decision and applies even where you are not terminally ill or permanently unconscious. It also applies in cases of temporary unconsciousness (if you were in an accident, for instance) or in cases of mental diseases like Alzheimer's disease which affects the decision-making process. The important point to remember is that it does not automatically terminate if you become incapacitated – in other words, it's durable!

With a healthcare power of attorney, you can specify guidelines and directions regarding the medical treatment that you want to receive during any period in which you are unable to make healthcare decisions on your own behalf. Save in the most extreme cases, your agent will be obliged to follow these instructions. You can also give your agent full freedom to make healthcare decisions on your behalf during any period in which you are incapacitated.

Ordinary and Durable Powers of Attorney

Apart from the above types of powers of attorney, powers of attorney can be categorized as either being ordinary or durable - both of which come to an end when the principal dies.

An ordinary power of attorney is only valid for as long as the principal is capable of making decisions and acting for him or herself. If the principal dies or becomes mentally incapacitated, the power of attorney is deemed invalid and immediately ceases to have effect. As a result, the family of the principal may be left in a position whereby they are powerless to deal with the principal's affairs unless they seek court intervention.

A durable power of attorney, on the other hand, remains valid even if the principal later becomes mentally incapacitated. In fact, the continuing validity of the agent's authorization after the principal becomes incapacitated is the significant difference between ordinary and durable powers of attorney.

To be recognized as durable, a power of attorney should contain a clear and unambiguous statement to the effect that it is intended to be 'durable'. It should also state that 'this power of attorney shall not be affected by the subsequent incapacity of the principal' or 'this power of attorney shall become effective upon the incapacity of the principal', as the case may be, or else use similar words that show it was intended to be valid even after the principal became incapacitated.

Springing Powers of Attorney

A 'springing' power of attorney is one that becomes effective at a future time. In other words, it 'springs' into effect when a defined event occurs, typically the incapacity of the principal.

Like most durable powers of attorney, it will contain a clause that provides that the principal's doctor will need to determine whether he or she is competent to handle his/her financial affairs before the authority will come into effect. Once it comes into effect, a springing power of attorney will continue until the principal's death, or until revoked by the court.

Mutual Powers of Attorney

Mutual powers of attorney are generally made between a husband and wife, and occasionally between the members of small businesses or professional firms. They serve as indicators of the mutual trust, confidence and the reliance that the parties enjoy within their relationship.

Each spouse or partner will appoint the other (or others) as their agent so as to ensure that their joint plans are implemented in the unfortunate event that one of them is rendered unable to act by illness or injury.

Cascading Powers of Attorney

A cascading power of attorney is simply a form of power of attorney which allows for the appointment of alternative or substitute agents or attorneys-in-fact. Its purpose is to provide for a backup in the situation where the first agent is unable or unwilling to act, and then further backups to replace the alternative attorneys-in-fact if they, too, decline to act, or cannot act for any reason.

Capacity to Make a Power of Attorney

Generally, anyone who has reached the age of majority in their state, who has sufficient mental capacity and who is not an un-discharged bankrupt can make a power of attorney. Even a company or a partnership can make a power of attorney.

The precise requirements for making a power of attorney differ from state to state. As such, if you are in any doubt as to whether you can make a power of attorney, you should seek the advice of a practicing attorney in your state.

What Does Being "Incapable" or "Incapacitated" Mean?

You will be deemed to be 'incapable' or 'incapacitated' if you are unable to understand and process information that is relevant to making an informed decision and if you are also unable to evaluate the likely consequences of making that decision.

The decision as to who determines whether you are incapacitated or not is generally set out in your power of attorney. Generally, a power of attorney will state that a doctor or attending physician must agree that you are incapable before you are actually deemed incapacitated and your power of attorney comes into effect.

While it may be somewhat obvious, it's worth pointing out that you must be mentally capable of granting a power of attorney at the time when the document was signed. This generally means that you must, if required, show that you are aware of the nature and extent of your assets and personal circumstances and that you understand your obligations in relation to your dependants and the nature of the power being granted to the agent under the power of attorney.

If you are found to be incapable or incapacitated in a time where you believe you are not, you have the right to request a capacity review hearing for the purpose of affirming or quashing that determination. You will have the right to be represented by counsel at that hearing. Agents appointed under a power of attorney have a general duty to explain this right to you and cannot try to prevent you from contacting a lawyer or asking for a review hearing. This said, it should be remembered that unless the agent is a professional accustomed to acting under a power of attorney, the likelihood is that the agent will not be aware of his obligation in this regard.

Should I Make a Power of Attorney?

The simple answer is yes! If you have an income or property of any description it's a good idea to execute a durable power of attorney especially if you believe that health problems may make it impossible for you to handle your personal financial affairs in the future. Even if you have no impending health issues, you should still have a durable power of attorney in case you, because of an accident or sudden illness, ever become unable to make decisions for yourself.

Have you ever considered what would happen if:-

- you were involved in a serious accident, which left you in a coma. What would your family do, in both the short and the longer term, if they had no power to access your bank accounts or take care of your business affairs?

- you began to have blackouts, and act in an out-of-character fashion. You're diagnosed as having a brain tumor, and before long you lose the capacity to function normally, or make rational decisions. Will your property, financial and other affairs be stuck in limbo?

In both of these cases, a durable power of attorney would be of great assistance to you. During your period of incapacity, your agent would be in a position to manage the many practical and financial tasks that may arise. For example, bills will need to be paid, bank deposits will need to be made, and someone will need to handle insurance and benefits paperwork, …..etc.

Many other matters may need attention as well, ranging from handling property repairs and lettings to managing investments or even a small business. In most cases, a durable general power of attorney is the best way to take care of all these and other similar tasks.

In addition, by preparing a power of attorney now, you can ensure that a person of your choosing will manage your property, assets and affairs rather than a court appointed conservator.

What Happens Without a Power of Attorney?

If you don't make a durable power of attorney, someone may have to be formally appointed by a court to make financial and other practical decisions (other than medical decisions) on your behalf. In essence, your family will have to make an application to court to have it make a determination that you cannot take care of your own affairs and request the court to make an order appointing a 'conservator' (also known as a guardian of the estate, committee, or curator) on your behalf. This application is often made in public and, in some instances, a notice of the intended application may even be published in a local newspaper. This can, as you will appreciate, be quite embarrassing and intrusive. Moreover, if family members disagree over who is to be appointed as the conservator or guardian, the proceedings may well become even more disagreeable and drawn out. The longevity of the proceedings can substantially increase the costs, especially as lawyers will need to be hired.

While the court will usually appoint a close family member to act as your conservator, it is under no obligation to do so. As such, it could end up appointing a complete stranger - someone who does not know you, who is not aware of your wishes, and who can legally ignore your family's requests and needs! For this reason alone, and forgetting the cost of such appointments, conservatorships are best avoided.

A conservator will generally need to:

- post a bond (a type of insurance policy) in case he or she steals or misuses your property;

- prepare (or hire a lawyer or accountant to prepare) detailed financial reports and periodically file them with the court; and

- get court approval before carrying out certain transactions, such as selling real estate or making investments.

The cost of these items all add up making conservatorships an expensive process; a process which ultimately needs to be paid from your estate. Appointing an agent under your power of attorney is, when done right, far more flexible and cheaper than a conservatorship and therefore an often favored alternative.

What if You Don't Think You Need a Power of Attorney?

You may not think that you need a durable power of attorney if, for example, you are married or if you have put the majority of your property and possessions into a living trust (also known as a family or inter vivos trust) or if you hold property as a joint tenant. However, the reality is that in all three of these instances, you will still need a durable general power of attorney if you become incapacitated.

Marriage

If you are married, your spouse will have a good degree of authority to deal with the property that you own together - for example, he or she will be able to continue to pay bills from a joint bank account or sell stocks or shares held in a joint brokerage account. However, there are very real restrictions on your spouse's ability to sell property owned by both of you. For example, in many states, one spouse cannot sell jointly owned real estate or automobiles without the consent of the other. If the other spouse is incapacitated and cannot give this consent, the sale cannot proceed. This may have important effects, particularly where the sales proceeds are required to pay on-going medical expenses or other important expenses.

In addition, when it comes to property in which your spouse has no legal interest, he or she will have no legal authority to deal with your assets in the absence of a durable power of attorney or court order.

Living Trusts

Even where you have a living trust, you should still consider making a power of attorney. In the majority of cases, the 'successor trustee' appointed under your living trust to distribute the trust property after your death also has the authority to take over management of the trust property during any period in which you become incapacitated. However, given that most people don't transfer all of their property into a living trust, a power of attorney should be made to cover any such property that's not so transferred.

Resource

For more information on living trusts, see our book entitled "Make Your Own Living Trust & Avoid Probate. See page 52.

Joint Tenancy

Joint tenancy is a form of joint ownership where each co-owner holds an undivided interest in the subject property. When one of the co-owners dies, the remaining co-owners automatically inherit the deceased's share of the property. While matters are relatively straight-forward in the case of death, they can become more complicated where one of the joint tenants becomes incapacitated. This is because the other joint tenants will have limited authority to deal with the joint tenancy property in the absence of being able to procure the consent of the incapacitated joint tenant. Real estate provides a good example of such a problem. If one owner becomes incapacitated, the others have no legal authority to sell or refinance the incapacitated owner's share of the property. By contrast, if the incapacitated joint owner had a durable power of attorney in place, they could give their agent authority to deal with their share of joint tenancy property and all matters relating to same, such as bank accounts, insurance and litigation. This would at least provide a means by which the assets could be legally dealt with and the rights of the co-owner exercised or enforced.

The Relationship Between Principal and Agent

One of the principal features underlying the relationship between a principal and an agent is the requirement that the agent acts with the utmost good faith on behalf of the principal. It is a relationship built on trust in which the agent is obliged to act with loyalty on behalf of the principal and in accordance with instructions received from the principal. The agent can neither intentionally ignore these instructions nor negligently act in the performance of them. In return for this loyalty, a principal instills confidence and trust in the agent thereby creating a fiduciary relationship of trust and confidence between the parties. It is this relationship of trust and confidence that underlies every specific action taken, or left untaken by the agent.

Unfortunately, human nature being what it is, the principles of trust upon which the fiduciary relationship is built are often honored more on paper than in observance. The reality is that people sometimes succumb to the pressure of other affairs, to a lack of thought about and appreciation of their obligations, and of course to temptation. This risk of breach is the primary risk associated with agency relationships particularly because of the agent's ability to bind the principal.

Who Can be an Agent?

While there is no need for an agent to be a lawyer or other professional person, he or she must be an adult capable of making decisions and carrying out specific tasks on your behalf. What's more, if the specific power of attorney you intend to create is one for healthcare, it may be advisable to weigh the agent's capacity for compassion as more valuable in this instance than their talents as a financial analyst or businessman.

The agent cannot be an un-discharged bankrupt and should not be the owner, operator or employee of a nursing home or extended care facility in which the principal is resident. Neither can the agent be a witness to your signature on the power of attorney.

Joint or Joint and Independent Agents

Sometimes a principal will want to appoint one or more agents to act on his/her behalf. Where the principal makes such a decision, he or she needs to decide whether the agents will be 'joint' agents or 'joint and independent' agents.

Joint agents must act together. As such, they must unanimously agree on a course of action before that action can proceed. Furthermore, in taking any action, joint agents must take the same action at the same time. For instance, if one of the agents is missing or unwilling to engage in a specific action, the remaining agents are powerless to act. This type of arrangement adds a degree of protection to the principal as it removes the possibility of any of the agents acting outside their instructions or in a 'rogue' capacity. 'Joint and independent' agents, on the other hand, can act either together or individually. As such, while both or all agents may be acting on behalf of the same principal and in relation to the same matter, they will not be obligated to consult with each other before taking an action which can bind the principal.

In the ordinary course of business, it is recommended that you avoid appointing joint agents. Rather, if more than one is to be appointed, it is preferable to appoint agents as alternates to the original agent.

Alternate Agents

While it is not necessary to do so, it is always a very good idea to appoint an alternate agent (also known as a substitute agent). The authority conferred on an alternate agent will only come into effect where the primary agent is unable or unwilling to act on behalf of the principal. In such circumstances, the alternate agent will acquire full power to act (unless expressly restricted) under the power of attorney.

In many cases, third parties (particularly financial institutions) will require proof that the original agent is unable or unwilling to act as agent under the power of attorney before accepting instructions from the alternate agent. In such cases, it's often useful for an alternate agent to request a signed confirmation from the principal revoking the authority of the original agent or, if available, from the original agent confirming in writing his or her refusal or inability to act as agent.

Scope of an Agent's Powers

Depending on whether the power of attorney is general or limited in nature, your agent will have as many or as few powers as you specify in the power of attorney. Within the scope of the authority you confer on your agent he or she can do anything that you can legally do.

You can give your agent authority to do some or all of the following:

(i)   use your assets to discharge the day-to-day expenses of you and your family;

(ii)   purchase, sell, lease, let, maintain, repair, pay taxes on and mortgage real estate and other property;

(iii)   claim and collect social insurance, government, civil, military and other entitlements;

(iv)   invest money in stocks, bonds and mutual funds;

(v)   effect transactions with financial institutions;

(vi)   buy, maintain and sell insurance policies and annuities;

(vii)   file and discharge your tax liabilities;

(viii) operate your small business;

(ix)   claim real estate or other property that you inherit or are otherwise entitled to;

(x)   transfer property into a trust you've created (if the rules of the trust permit);

(xi)   engage someone to represent you in court or to run legal actions on your behalf; and

(xii)   manage your affairs generally.

Note that the above list is not exhaustive.

Duties and Responsibilities of an Agent

Generally speaking, your agent has the following primary duties and responsibilities:

- to act in your best interest;

- to keep accurate records of dealings/transactions undertaken on your behalf;

- to act towards you with the utmost good faith and to avoid situations where there is a conflict of interest; and

- to keep your property and money separate from their own.

As far as keeping accurate records is concerned, the agent should keep a list or register of:

- all the principal's assets as at the date of his first transaction;

- all assets acquired and disposed of and the date and particulars of each such transaction;

- all receipts and disbursements and the date and particulars of each such transaction;

- all investments bought and sold and the date and particulars of each such transaction;

- all the principal's liabilities as of the date of the agent's first transaction;

- all liabilities incurred and paid and the date and particulars of each such transaction; and

- all compensation taken by the agent and the manner in which it was calculated.

Your agent should keep these records until he or she ceases acting for you and until the date upon which he or she is relieved from acting as your agent. These records should be handed over to either the agent's successor, or if the power of attorney terminates by reason of the principal's death or otherwise, to the principal's legal personal representative. Of course, if the principal has merely recovered from an incapacity, the records can be given back to the principal directly.

Choosing an Agent

Your agent will be acting on your behalf, as such, the person you choose should obviously be someone you know and trust thoroughly. In making any decisions, you must bear in mind that your agent will have complete authority to deal with your financial and legal affairs (subject to any limitations or restrictions specified in your power of attorney).

You should ensure that the person you choose has adequate financial management skills and sufficient time to handle your affairs properly. Your agent must be available when required, be able to objectively make decisions and be able to keep accurate financial records.

What Laws Govern My Power of Attorney?

A power of attorney is normally governed by the law specified in the document itself or by the law of the jurisdiction in which the actions of the agent are to be performed. Normally, this is the place in which the property or assets of the principal are located. For this reason, it makes sense to appoint an agent located in that specific jurisdiction. If you anticipate that your agent will be acting in more than one jurisdiction, you should consider making separate powers of attorney for each jurisdiction.

A jurisdiction is essentially a place that has its own laws. Among others, this can be a county, a state or a country.

If your power of attorney is to be used in a foreign country, you may have to have it "authenticated" or "legalized" before it can lawfully be used. This is a process whereby a government official certifies that the signature of the authority (usually a notary or lawyer) on your document is authentic and, as such, should be accepted in the foreign country. For more information about document authentication and legalization, contact the local consulate/embassy of the foreign country in which you propose your power of attorney to be used.

Most jurisdictions have their own power of attorney forms, but it's generally not mandatory that you use them. For example, lawyers frequently prepare powers of attorney for their clients using their standard terminology rather than adopting state approved forms. As long as the document is headed 'power of attorney', specifies the parties, is signed and dated, and contains recognizable terms normally found in a power of attorney, it should be accepted by most authorities and organizations as such.

In addition to law firms, banks and brokerage houses often have their own power of attorney forms too. If you want to ensure that your agent can transact business on your behalf with these institutions, you should consider preparing two (or more) powers of attorney — one being your own form and the others being those required by the institutions with which you propose to do business through your agent. You should obviously check with the relevant institutions in advance, to ascertain their specific requirements, and even obtain copies of the forms they prefer to use. That way, you can fill in and sign their form at the same time as you prepare and execute your 'general purpose' power of attorney.

In terms of signing and witnessing, different jurisdictions tend to have different requirements for powers of attorney. These requirements can vary depending on the powers to be conferred on the agent and the type of power of attorney you are executing. As such, you will need to check the laws applicable in your state to see how your power of attorney should be executed. In most cases, however, executing your power of attorney in front of a witness or a notary will suffice.

Witness to a Power of Attorney

Capacity to Make a Power of Attorney To satisfy various jurisdictional requirements, it is advisable that you not use any of the following people as your witnesses:

- your spouse;

- your partner;

- your child;

- your agent or alternate agent;

- the spouse of your agent or alternate agent; or

- employees of a medical facility in which you are a patient.

Your witnesses must be of legal age in your state. They must also have legal capacity and be of sound mind.

Commencement of a Power of Attorney

A power of attorney will start on a date specified in the document or, in some cases, upon the occurrence of a specified event. If there is no specified date or event, a power of attorney starts immediately upon notification to the agent, following its execution by the principal and appropriate witnessing.

A durable power of attorney can be drafted to start at either the time of its signing, or upon the incapacity of the principal.

Filing or Recording a Power of Attorney

Normally, powers of attorney do not require legal registration to become operative. However, where your agent will be acting in relation to any sort of land transaction, a power of attorney will usually need to be recorded or filed with the County Clerk or the Land Titles Office (the exact filing authority depending on the jurisdiction). If this is the case, the document will probably also need to be notarized.

When you register the document is largely up to you as there are generally no time requirements for registration. If it's not needed straight away, and you don't want the document placed on public record straight away, you can hold off on registering it until it's needed. When the time comes, your agent can then register it. However, if you are adopting this approach, you need to check with the clerk in the registry of deeds to see what the specific requirements are for registering. For example, in some states, the documents must be a specific size or on specific types of paper. Assuming that your document meets the required standards, you can then choose to wait before registering.

If you intend to register your document in the Registry of Deeds in Illinois, Indiana, Kentucky or Minnesota you will also need to complete the "Preparation Statement" section at the end of the power of attorney document at the back of this kit. This section simply identifies the person who has prepared the document. In most cases, this will be you (the principal). However, if someone has prepared it on your behalf, they should be identified in this section.

Revocation of a Power of Attorney

Provided you are not incapacitated, you can revoke a power of attorney at any time by sending a 'notice of revocation of a power of attorney' to your agent. This is a written legal notice signed by or on behalf of a person who granted a power of attorney stating that he or she is terminating the powers conferred on the agent under an earlier power of attorney.

There are a number of reasons, practical and personal, why you might want to revoke your power of attorney. These may be that:

- the power of attorney is no longer necessary as you are now able to act on your own behalf;

- you no longer trust the agent who is acting on your behalf;

- you have found a more suitable person to act as your agent;

- it is no longer practical to have your agent acting on your behalf; and

- the purpose behind originally granting the power of attorney has been fulfilled and you no longer need an agent to act on your behalf.

The revocation of a power of attorney is not effective against the agent or any third party who may rely on it until such time that notice of the revocation has been received by that party. As such, it is common practice to have a written notice evidencing the revocation rather than simply trying to revoke the authority orally. This written document can, in turn, be sent (by recorded delivery, if necessary) to all third parties who may rely on the power of attorney to put them on notice that your agent's authority has been revoked.

Important Points & Recommendation

While a power of attorney can be an exceptionally handy tool, it is important to remember that it is a serious legal document with far-reaching consequences. Therefore drawing up and signing a power of attorney is something that you should not do without due care and forethought. And while you can pick up a power of attorney form online or at a business supply store and then fill it out yourself, you should be cautious about the forms you use. Indeed you should only use forms from reputable vendors such as Enodare. If you are in any doubt as to the adequacy of the forms or what they do, speak to a lawyer before using them.

MAKE YOUR OWN DURABLE LIMITED POWER OF ATTORNEY

Now that you understand what a power of attorney is, how it operates in practice and the importance of having one, it's time for you to consider making your own. At the back of this kit, we have included a sample durable limited power of attorney form. A brief description of this durable limited power of attorney form is set out below:

- Has limited scope and only covers a limited section of your legal and financial affairs. You are free to choose the scope of your agent's authority.

- Agent's authority commences either on signing or following a medical determination that you have become incapacitated.

- Agent's authority terminates (i) when you revoke your agent's authority, (ii) on your death, (iii) on a specific date or (iv) on the occurrence of a specific event.

- Not terminated by incapacity and operates during any period in which you are incapacitated.

We have also included a Notice of Revocation of a Power of Attorney and an Agent's Acceptance of Appointment at the back of this kit for your convenience.

Before using any of the forms in this kit, you should carefully review them in order to ensure that they meet your requirements and are suitable having regard to your particular circumstances. If you are in any doubt as to the suitability of the documents for your use or the scope of the documents, you should consult an attorney before using these documents. If you decide to use any of the above mentioned documents, be sure to read the document in full and follow the signing instructions carefully. Remember, these documents are provided on an 'as-is' basis and the decision to use them is yours.

IMPORTANT NOTICE

This document will give the person you name as your agent the power to make legal/financial decisions on your behalf. This power is subject to any limitations that you expressly include in your document. After you have signed this document, you will still have the right and authority to make financial decisions for yourself if you are mentally competent to do so.

APPENDIX 1

SIGNING INSTRUCTIONS

Instructions for Completion of the Durable Limited Power of Attorney Document

1. Carefully read all the instructions below.

2. Print out the document which you intend using and complete it neatly using a pen or carefully edit the text version of the form (that is available to you to download) on your computer.

3. On the cover page of the document, insert the date of execution of the power of attorney as well as your name, as principal, in the spaces provided.

4. Clause 1 identifies the parties to the power of attorney. In this clause, you will need to enter (i) your name and address, (ii) that of your primary agent and (iii) that of your alternate agent in the spaces provided.

5. In Clause 2, specify the maximum duration for which your agent will be entitled to act on your behalf under the power of attorney.

6. In Clause 3, you will need to decide whether you would like your power of attorney to (i) take effect immediately, in which case your agent can immediately commence acting for you; or (ii) only come into effect when you are deemed to be mentally incapacitated by a doctor. If you would prefer option (i), then initial the first paragraph of this clause in the space provided. If you would prefer option (ii), then initial the second paragraph of this clause in the space provided.

   If you select option (ii) and initial the second paragraph, you will also need to add the name and address of a physician in the third paragraph. This will be the physician that you would prefer to have examine you in order to determine whether or not you are mentally incapacitated.

7. In Clause 4, specify the purpose(s) for which the power of attorney is being granted. E.g. "carrying out real estate transactions" or "purchasing a detached office property located at 123 Little Street, Small Town for the sum of $250,000 from John Smith". Be as specific and concise as possible.

8. In Clause 11, enter your state of residence.

9. Arrange to meet with a notary. Once you meet the notary, you should proceed to step 10 – in the notary's presence.

10. In the execution block, immediately after Clause 11, enter the date, month, year and place of execution. Then sign your name on the signature line above the words "The Principal" in the presence of the notary and two witnesses.

    Your witnesses should not be a person who is:

    - your agent or attorney-in-fact;

    - the notary acknowledging your signature;

    - a relation by blood, marriage, or adoption to you or your agent; or a spouse of any such person;

    - financially responsible for your medical care;

    - entitled to any portion of your estate following your death;

    - a beneficiary under an insurance policy on your life;

    - entitled to make a claim against your estate (such as creditors); or

    - your attending physician, nor an employee of such a physician.

11. You should have the two witnesses who witnessed your execution of the power of attorney complete the "Witness Affidavit" section of the document.

12. You should then have a notary complete the "Notary Affidavit" section of the document.

13. If you intend to register your document in the Registry of Deeds in Illinois, Indiana, Kentucky or Minnesota you will need to complete the "Preparation Statement" section of the document. This section simply identifies the person who has prepared the document. In most cases, this will be you (the principal). However, if someone has prepared it on your behalf, they should be identified in this section.

14. If you live in California, Georgia, Montana, New Hampshire, Pennsylvania, Vermont or Wisconsin you will need to have your agent accept his or her appointment under the power of attorney before they can lawfully act. You can do this by having your agent complete and sign the Acknowledgement of Agent section of the document.

In fact, while there is no obligation to do so, it is both recommended and good practice to always get your agent to sign this acknowledgement irrespective of what state you reside it.

In Georgia, you will also need to have your agent complete the Agent's Acceptance of Appointment document in Appendix 3 and attach it to your power of attorney document.

15. If you are making a power of attorney for use in either of North Carolina or South Carolina, then you must record it with the registry of deeds before it can be deemed to be durable. Similarly, if your power of attorney is to grant authority over real property to your agent, it should also be registered in the registry of deeds otherwise your agent may not be deemed to have authority to deal with your real property.

When you register the document is largely up to you as there are generally no time requirements for registration. If it's not needed straight away, and you don't want the document placed on public record straight away, you can hold off on registering it until it's needed. When the time comes, your agent can then register it. However, if you are adopting this approach, you need to check with the clerk in the registry of deeds to see what the specific requirements are for registering. For example, in some states, the documents must be a specific size or on specific types of paper. Assuming that your document meets the required standards, you can then choose to wait before registering.

Instructions for Completion of the Agent's Acceptance of Appointment Document

1. Carefully read all the instructions below.

2. Print out the document which you intend using and complete it neatly using a pen or carefully edit the text version of the form (that is available to you to download) on your computer.

3. The first paragraph identifies the agent and the principal. Therefore, in this paragraph, you will need to enter (i) the name of your agent and (ii) that of the principal in the spaces provided. Your agent will then need to date and sign the document at the bottom of the page, as well as specify his address.

4. If the power of attorney document grants the agent authority to deal with real estate, the agent should sign the document in front of a notary.

Instructions for Completion of the Notice of Revocation of a Power of Attorney Document

1. Carefully read all the instructions below.

2. Print out the document which you intend using and complete it neatly using a pen or carefully edit the text version of the form (that is available to you to downlad) on your computer.

3. On the cover page of the document, insert the date of execution of the notice of revocation as well as your name, as principal, in the spaces provided.

4. The first paragraph of the document identifies the parties to the original power of attorney and its date. In this paragraph, you will need to enter (i) your name and address, (ii) the date of the power of attorney and (iii) the name of your agent.

5. Arrange to meet with a notary. Once you meet the notary, you should proceed to step 6 – in the notary's presence.

6. In the execution block, enter the date, month, year, and place of execution. Then sign your name on the signature line above the words "The Principal" in the presence of the notary and two witnesses.

    Your witnesses should not be a person who is:

    *   your agent or attorney-in-fact;

    *   the notary acknowledging your signature;

    *   a relation by blood, marriage, or adoption to you or your agent; or a spouse of any such person;

    *   financially responsible for your medical care;

    *   entitled to any portion of your estate following your death;

    *   a beneficiary under an insurance policy on your life;

    *   entitled to make a claim against your estate (such as creditors); or

- your attending physician, nor an employee of such a physician.

7. You should have the two witnesses who witnessed your execution of the notice of revocation complete the "Witness Affidavit" section of the document.

8. You should then have a notary complete the "Notary Affidavit" section of the document.

APPENDIX 2

SAMPLE

DURABLE LIMITED POWER OF ATTORNEY
FOR FINANCE AND PROPERTY

Downloadable Forms

Blank copies of this form are available to download from our website.

Web: http://www.enodare.com/downloadarea/

Unlock Code: CHP36756

enodare

DATED THIS ____ DAY OF _____, 20___.

_____

DURABLE LIMITED POWER OF ATTORNEY

of

_____

(Principal)

_____

NOTICE: THE POWERS GRANTED BY THIS DOCUMENT MAY BE BROAD AND SWEEPING. IF YOU HAVE ANY QUESTIONS ABOUT THESE POWERS, OBTAIN COMPETENT LEGAL ADVICE. THIS DOCUMENT DOES NOT AUTHORIZE ANYONE TO MAKE MEDICAL AND OTHER HEALTHCARE DECISIONS FOR YOU. YOU MAY REVOKE THIS POWER OF ATTORNEY IF YOU LATER WISH TO DO SO PROVIDED YOU ARE OF SOUND MIND.

DURABLE LIMITED POWER OF ATTORNEY

1.   I, _____ of _____
_____ aged eighteen years and upwards hereby appoint
_____ of _____
_ as my lawfully appointed attorney in fact (referred to as the "Agent") on
and subject to the terms and conditions set out below. If for any reason this
person shall be unable or unwilling to act as my Agent, I hereby appoint
_____ of _____
__ to act as my Agent instead subject to the terms and conditions set out
herein.

2.   This durable limited power of attorney shall apply for financial and
property applications only, shall not be affected by my subsequent disability
or incapacity and shall remain effective until the earlier of (i) _____ days
from the date hereof; (ii) the date of any written revocation of my Agent's
authority hereunder; (iii) the date upon which my Agent has fulfilled the
purpose set out in Clause 4 hereof; or (iv) the date of my death.

3.   I direct that this durable limited power of attorney shall become effective in
the manner that I have expressed below:-

(initial only one option below)

_____   This durable power of attorney is hereby effective immediately
and shall continue in full force and effect until it is terminated in
accordance with Clause 2 hereof. This power of attorney shall
be construed as a durable limited power of attorney and shall
continue to be effective even if I become disabled, incapacitated, or
incompetent.

_____   This durable power of attorney shall, subject to Clause 2, become
effective only in the event that I become mentally incapacitated or
disabled so that as a result I am not able to manage my financial
affairs in which case it shall become effective as of the date of
the written statement to be provided by a physician pursuant to
the terms of this Clause 3. If this power of attorney becomes
effective, it shall remain effective during any period in which I am
incapacitated or disabled until terminated in accordance with Clause
2.

The determination of whether I have become incapacitated or disabled so that I am not able to manage my financial affairs shall be made in writing by a licensed physician; if practical, this physician shall be _____ of _____ _____ or failing him/her any licensed physician having been at least ten years in practice.

In the event that a licensed physician has made a written determination pursuant to this Clause 3 that I have become incapacitated or disabled and as a result unable to manage my own financial affairs, such written statement shall be attached to the original of this power of attorney.

4.   I hereby grant (subject to the provisions of Clause 5) my Agent full power and authority to do and perform each and every act which I could do or perform for the purpose(s) of _____

_____

_____

_____

_____ and I hereby ratify and confirm all that my Agent shall do or cause to be done under this power of attorney.

5.   My Agent shall have no authority to give any of my property to, or use any of my property for the benefit of himself or herself. In addition, my agent (i) cannot execute a will, a codicil, or any will substitute on my behalf; (ii) cannot change the beneficiary on any life insurance policy that I own; (iii) cannot make gifts on my behalf; (iv) may not exercise any powers that would cause any assets of mine to be considered taxable to my Agent or to my Agent's estate for purposes of any income, estate, or inheritance tax, and (v) cannot contravene any medical or healthcare power of attorney or living will I have executed whether prior or subsequent to the execution of this power of attorney.

6.   The powers conferred on my Agent herein may be exercised by my Agent alone, and my Agent's signature or act under the authority granted herein may be accepted by any third person or organization as fully authorized by me and with the same legal force and effect as if I were personally present, competent and acting on my own behalf.

7.   Third parties may rely upon the representations of the Agent as to all

matters regarding powers granted to the Agent. No person who acts in reliance on the authority granted under this power of attorney shall incur any liability to me or to my estate for permitting the Agent to exercise any power prior to actual knowledge that the power of attorney has been revoked or terminated by operation of law or otherwise.

8. No agent named or substituted in this power of attorney shall incur any liability to me for acting or refraining from acting under this power, except for such agent's own misconduct, fraud or negligence.

9. My Agent shall provide an accounting for all funds and assets handled and all acts performed as my Agent, if I so request or if such a request is made by any authorized personal representative or fiduciary properly acting on my behalf. My Agent shall not however be obliged to file any such accountings or any inventory with a court and any obligation in this respect is hereby waived to the fullest extent permitted by law.

10. My Agent shall be reimbursed for reasonable expenses incurred while acting as my Agent and may receive reasonable compensation for acting as Agent.

11. This power of attorney will be governed by the laws of the State of _____ without regard for conflicts of laws principles and is intended to be valid in all jurisdictions of the United States of America and all foreign nations.

Executed this _____ day of _____, 20_____, at _____ _____.

_____

The Principal

WITNESS AFFIDAVIT

I declare, on the basis of information and belief, that the person who signed or acknowledged this document (the "principal") is personally known to me, that he/she signed or acknowledged this Power of Attorney in my presence, and that he/she appears to be of sound mind and under no duress, fraud, or undue influence. I am not related to the principal by blood, marriage, or adoption, either as a spouse, a lineal ancestor, descendant of the parents of the principal, or spouse of any of them. I am not directly financially responsible for the principal's medical care. I am not entitled to any portion of the principal's estate upon his/her decease, whether under any Will or as an heir by intestate succession, nor am I the beneficiary of an insurance policy on the principal's life, nor do I have a claim against the principal's estate as of this time. I am not the principal's attending physician, nor an employee of the attending physician. No more than one witness is an employee of a health facility in which the principal is a patient. I am not appointed as healthcare agent or successor healthcare agent by this document.

Witness No. 1

Signature: _____

Date: _____

Print Name: _____

Telephone: _____

Residence Address: _____

_____

_____

_____

Signature: _____

Date: _____

Print Name: _____

Telephone: _____

Residence Address: _____

_____

_____

_____

NOTARY AFFIDAVIT

STATE OF _____   **COUNTY OF** _____

On _____ before me, _____, a notary public, personally appeared _____, who proved to me on the basis of satisfactory evidence to be the person whose name is subscribed to the within instrument and acknowledged to me that he/she executed the same in his/her authorized capacity, and that by his/her signature on the instrument he/she executed the instrument. I certify under PENALTY OF PERJURY that the foregoing is true and correct. Witness my hand and official seal.

Signature: _____

Print Name: _____

My commission expires on: _____

(Seal)

PREPARATION STATEMENT

This document was prepared by the following individual:

_____

Print Name

_____

Signature

ACKNOWLEDGMENT OF AGENT

BY ACCEPTING OR ACTING UNDER THE APPOINTMENT, THE AGENT ASSUMES THE FIDUCIARY AND OTHER LEGAL RESPONSIBILITIES OF AN AGENT.

_____

Print Name of Agent

_____

Signature of Agent

APPENDIX 3

AGENT'S ACCEPTANCE OF APPOINTMENT

(FOR USE IN GEORGIA ONLY)

Appendix 3

ACCEPTANCE OF APPOINTMENT

I, _____ (print name), have read the foregoing
Power of Attorney and am the person identified therein as Agent for
_____ (name of grantor of power of attorney), the Principal
named therein. I hereby acknowledge the following:

(i)   I owe a duty of loyalty and good faith to the Principal, and must use the powers granted to me only for the benefit of the Principal.

(ii)   I must keep the Principal's funds and other assets separate and apart from my funds and other assets and titled in the name of the Principal. I must not transfer title to any of the Principal's funds or other assets into my name alone. My name must not be added to the title of any funds or other assets of the Principal, unless I am specifically designated as Agent for the Principal in the title.

(iii)   I must protect, conserve, and exercise prudence and caution in my dealings with the Principal's funds and other assets.

(iv)   I must keep a full and accurate record of my acts, receipts, and disbursements on behalf of the Principal, and be ready to account to the Principal for such acts, receipts, and disbursements at all times. I must provide an annual accounting to the Principal of my acts, receipts, and disbursements, and must furnish an accounting of such acts, receipts, and disbursements to the personal representative of the Principal's estate within 90 days after the date of death of the Principal.

I have read the Compensation of Agent paragraph in the Power of Attorney and agree to abide by it.

I acknowledge my authority to act on behalf of the Principal ceases at the death of the Principal.

I hereby accept the foregoing appointment as Agent for the Principal with full knowledge of the responsibilities imposed on me, and I will faithfully carry out my duties to the best of my ability.

Dated:_____, _____.

(Signature)_____

(Address)_____

Note: A notarized signature is not required unless the Principal has included instructions regarding property transactions.

I, _____, a Notary Public, do hereby certify that _____ personally appeared before me this date and acknowledged the due execution of the foregoing Acceptance of Appointment.

_____

Notary Public

APPENDIX 4

NOTICE OF REVOCATION
OF A POWER OF ATTORNEY

Downloadable Forms

Blank copies of this form are available to download from our website.

Web: http://www.enodare.com/downloadarea/

Unlock Code: CHP36756

enodare

DATED THIS ____ DAY OF _____, 20___.

NOTICE OF REVOCATION

of

_____

(Principal)

www.enodare.com

NOTICE OF REVOCATION

I, _____ of _____

_____

aged eighteen years and upwards hereby revoke, countermand and make null and void the Power of Attorney dated _____ (the "Power of Attorney") and granted in favor of _____ (the "Agent", which expression shall include any successor agent appointed under the Power of Attorney) and all rights, powers and authority thereby given to the Agent shall hereby lapse and cease.

Executed this _____ day of _____,
20 _____, at _____.

_____
THE PRINCIPAL

WITNESS AFFIDAVIT

I declare, on the basis of information and belief, that the person who signed or acknowledged this document (the "principal") is personally known to me, that he/she signed or acknowledged this Notice of Revocation of a Power of Attorney in my presence, and that he/she appears to be of sound mind and under no duress, fraud, or undue influence. I am not related to the principal by blood, marriage, or adoption, either as a spouse, a lineal ancestor, descendant of the parents of the principal, or spouse of any of them. I am not directly financially responsible for the principal's medical care. I am not entitled to any portion of the principal's estate upon his/her decease, whether under any Will or as an heir by intestate succession, nor am I the beneficiary of an insurance policy on the principal's life, nor do I have a claim against the principal's estate as of this time. I am not the principal's attending physician, nor an employee of the attending physician. No more than one witness is an employee of a health facility in which the principal is a patient. I am not appointed as healthcare agent or successor healthcare agent by this document.

Witness No. 1

Signature: _____

Date: _____

Print Name: _____

Telephone: _____

Residence Address: _____

_____

_____

_____

Witness No. 2

Signature: _____

Date: _____

Print Name: _____

Telephone: _____

Residence Address: _____

_____

_____

_____

NOTARY AFFIDAVIT

STATE OF _____   **COUNTY OF** _____

On _____ before me, _____, a notary public, personally appeared _____, who proved to me on the basis of satisfactory evidence to be the person whose name is subscribed to the within instrument and acknowledged to me that he/she executed the same in his/her authorized capacity, and that by his/her signature on the instrument he/she executed the instrument. I certify under PENALTY OF PERJURY that the foregoing is true and correct. Witness my hand and official seal.

Signature: _____

Print Name: _____

My commission expires on: _____

(Seal)

Other Great Books from Enodare's Estate Planning Series

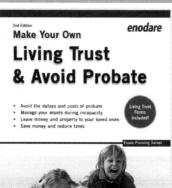
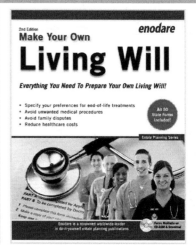

Make Your Own Last Will & Testament

By making a will, you can provide for the distribution of your assets to your love ones, appoint guardians to care for your children, provide for the management of gifts to young adults and children, specify how your debts are to be paid following your death, make funeral arrangements and much more.

This book will guide you through the entire process of making a will. It contains all the forms that you will need to make a valid legal will, simply and easily.

Make Your Own Living Trust & Avoid Probate

Living trusts are used to distribute a person's assets after they die in a manner that avoids the costs, delays and publicity of probate. They also cater for the management of property during periods of incapacity.

This book will guide you step-by-step through the process of creating your very own living trust, transferring assets to your living trust and subsequently managing those assets.

All relevant forms are included.

Make Your Own Living Will

Do you want a say in what life sustaining medical treatments you receive during periods in which you are incapacitated and either in a permanent state of unconsciousness or suffering from a terminal illness? Well if so, you must have a living will!

This book will introduce you to living wills, the types of medical procedures that they cover, the matters that you need to consider when making them and, of course, provide you with all the relevant forms you need to make your own living will!

www.enodare.com

Other Great Books from Enodare's Estate Planning Series

Estate Planning Essentials	How to Probate an Estate - A Step-By-Step Guide for Executors	Funeral Planning Basics - A Step-By-Step Guide to Funeral Planning

Estate Planning Essentials

This book is a must read for anyone who doesn't already have a comprehensive estate plan.

It will show you the importance of having wills, trusts, powers of attorney and living wills in your estate plan. You will learn about the probate process, why people are so keen to avoid it and lots of simple methods you can actually use to do so. You will learn about reducing estate taxes and how best to provide for young beneficiaries and children.

This book is a great way to get you started on the way to making your own estate plan.

How to Probate an Estate - A Step-By-Step Guide for Executors

This book is essential reading for anyone contemplating acting as an executor of someone's estate!

Learn about the various stages of probate and what an executor needs to do at each stage to successfully navigate his way through to closing the estate and distributing the deceased's assets.

You will learn how an executor initiates probate, locates and manages assets, deals with debt and taxes, distributes assets, and much more. This is a fantastic step-by-step guide through the entire process!

Funeral Planning Basics - A Step-By-Step Guide to Funeral Planning

Through proper funeral planning, you can ensure that your loved ones are not confronted with the unnecessary burden of having to plan a funeral at a time which is already very traumatic for them.

This book will introduce you to issues such as organ donations, purchasing caskets, cremation, burial, purchasing grave plots, organization of funeral services, legal and financial issues, costs of pre-arranging a funeral, how to save money on funerals, how to finance funerals and much more.

www.enodare.com

Will Writer - Estate Planning Software

Everything You Need to Create Your Estate Plan

Product Description

Enodare's Estate Planning Software helps you create wills, living trusts, living wills, powers of attorney and more from the comfort of your own home and without the staggering legal fees!

Through the use of a simple question and answer process, we'll guide you step-by-step through the process of preparing your chosen document. It only takes a few minutes of your time and comprehensive help and information is available at every stage of the process.

Product Features:

 ### Last Wills

Make gifts to your family, friends and charities, make funeral arrangements, appoint executors, appoint guardians to care for your minor children, make property management arrangements for young beneficiaries, release people from debts, and much more.

 ### Living Trusts

Make gifts to your family and friends, make property management arrangements for young beneficiaries, transfer assets tax efficiently with AB Trusts, and much more.

 ### Living Wills

Instruct doctors as to your choices regarding the receipt or non-receipt of medical treatments designed to prolong your life.

Healthcare Power of Attorney

Appoint someone you trust to make medical decisions for you if you become mentally incapacitated.

 ### Power of Attorney for Finance and Property

Appoint someone you trust to manage your financial affairs if you become mentally incapacitated, or if you are unable to do so for any reason.

 ### And More.........

Enodare's Will Writer software also includes documents such as self proving Affidavits, Deeds of Assignment, Certifications of Trust, Estate Planning Worksheet, Revocation forms and more.

The documents are valid in all states except Louisiana.

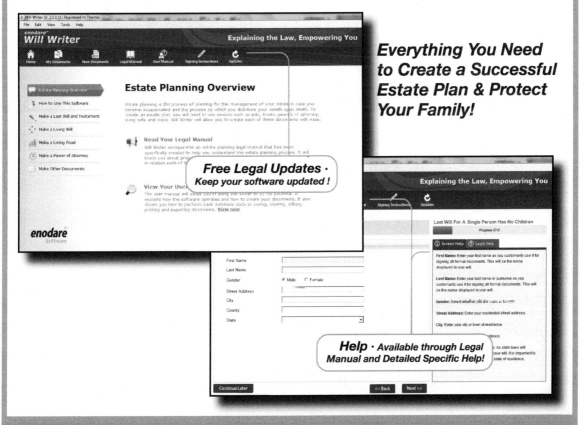

Everything You Need to Create a Successful Estate Plan & Protect Your Family!

Entrepreneur's Guide to Starting a Business

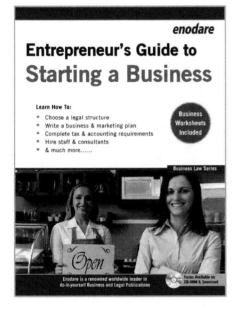

Entrepreneur's Guide to Starting a Business takes the fear of the unknown out of starting your new business and provides a treasure chest of information that will help you be successful from the very start.

First-time entrepreneurs face a daunting challenge in identifying all of the issues that must be addressed and mastered when starting a new business. If any item slips through the cracks, or is handled improperly, it could bring a new company crashing to the ground. Entrepreneur's Guide to Starting a Business helps you meet that challenge by walking you through all of the important aspects of successfully launching your own business.

When you finish reading this book, not alone will you know the step-by-step process needed to turn your business idea and vision into a successful reality, but you'll also have a wealth of practical knowledge about corporate structures, business & marketing plans, e-commerce, hiring staff & external advisors, finding commercial property, sales & marketing, legal & financial matters, tax and much more.

- Comprehensive overview of all major aspects of starting a new business

- Covers every stage of the process, from writing your business plan to marketing and selling your new product

- Plain English descriptions of complex subject matters

- Real-world case study showing you how things play out in an actual new business environment

NEW TITLE

Personal Budget Kit

Budgeting Made Easy

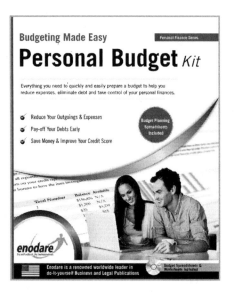

In this kit, we'll guide you step-by-step through the process of creating and living with a personal budget. We'll show you how analyze how you receive and spend your money and to set goals, both short and long-term.

You'll learn how to gain control of your personal cash flow. You'll discover when you need to make adjustments to your budget and how to do it wisely. Most of all, this kit will show you that budgeting isn't simply about adding limitations to your living but rather the foundation for living better by maximizing the resources you have.

This Personal Budget Kit provides you with step-by-step instructions, detailed information and all the budget worksheets and spreadsheets necessary to identify and understand your spending habits, reduce your expenses, set goals, prepare personal budgets, monitor your progress and take control over your finances.

- Reduce your spending painlessly and effortlessly

- Pay off your debts early

- Improve your credit rating

- Save & invest money

- Set & achieve financial goals

- Eliminate financial worries

Budget Planning Spreadsheets Included

enodare

NEW TITLE